INHERITANCE

Born in South London in 1937, Paul Bailey won a scholarship to the Central School of Speech and Drama in 1953 and later worked as an actor. His novels include *At the Jerusalem* (1967; reissued 2019) and, most recently, *Chapman's Odyssey* (2011) and *The Prince's Boy* (2014). *Peter Smart's Confessions* (1977) and *Gabriel's Lament* (1986) were both shortlisted for the Booker Prize. His other work has included an 'alternative biography' of Fred Barnes, Naomi Jacob and Arthur Marshall (*Three Queer Lives*); books about Quentin Crisp and Cynthia Payne; two volumes of memoirs; and plays for radio and television.

PAUL BAILEY

Inheritance

First published in 2019
by CB editions
146 Percy Road London W12 9QL
www.cbeditions.com

Printed in England by Blissetts, London W3 8DH

ISBN 978–1–909585–30–0

For Jeremy

ACKNOWLEDGEMENTS

Some of these poems first appeared in the *Times Literary Supplement*. Grateful thanks are due to Alan Jenkins and the late Mick Imlah. 'Three Scenes from the Midwest' was published in *London Magazine*, under the editorship of the unforgotten Alan Ross. Dr Steven Jacobi, Head of English at Wellington College International, Shanghai, chose the poem 'Summer of Love' for inclusion in a special edition of the college's magazine *The Retreat*, devoted entirely to the *Star Wars* films. I offer him my surprised and delighted thanks.

The poem 'Essential Stationery' is dedicated to Maggi Hambling; 'Urban' to Marius Chivu, and 'Lyrical' to Norman and Cella Manea.

I want to thank the following dear friends for their sometimes critical encouragement: Georgina Hammick, in particular; Ali Smith and Sarah Wood; Peter Parker; David Perry; Shena Mackay; Sarah Hutchings and Hilary Cooke and Roger and Anna Lewis.

Two people especially have made the publication of this collection possible. Matthew Marland, the young agent I acquired following the shocking death of his much loved predecessor David Miller, at Rogers, Coleridge & White, has been a tireless enthusiast for my poetry. He has made himself quietly and humorously effectual on my behalf. Finally, I have to express my gratitude to Charles Boyle, founder of the wonderfully individual publishing house CB editions. He is one of the shrewdest and least dictatorial editors I have ever worked with. He is publishing this book because he wants to and that is a great honour.

'Inheritance' is dedicated to a long-suffering and exceptional human being.

There is nothing fine about being a child; it is fine, when we are old, to look back to when we were children.

– Cesare Pavese, *This Business of Living*

Contents

For J.

This coming-together, this sweetness,
this stopping-of-clocks for unwatched hours
might be the gift of grief:
a blessing from two ghosts.

Such a warm union of eyes and hands –
now focused, now attached –
might be their benison:
our somewhere from their nowhere.

Your hair looks startled after sleep.
My morning's task's to calm it.
This is a gesture that might not have been
without their absence.

Inheritance

Despair's a curious thing to give a child.
It was my father's gift to me
times beyond numbering.

He gave it casually, in frowns and sighs,
with never any cause for decoration
or fancy wrapping.

His silences were like fugues to me,
their resonance composed of other silences
too terrible for voicing.

That was his way with his youngest son
who had battled for life at the age of four
and was still surviving.

He'd earned his gloom in Flanders, in the mud.
This much I learned on his last night alive
when he couldn't stop talking.

Lullaby

An illness took my voice away.
I listened and I listened and I listened
to catch each precious word I couldn't speak.

The nurses spoke to me and sang to me
welcoming me back with gentleness
to where I was before the stone lodged in my throat.

'This little boy deserves a lullaby,' the matron said.
'See that he gets one every night.'
The nurses, Joan and Mabel, honoured her command.

My voice returned to me, making a purer sound.
I was released into the world of speech once more,
hoping to hear a lullaby again.

Gaiety

Some people are sustained by sorrow.
I think I'm one of them.
That's why I laugh so much.
That's why I'm called a clown.
And that's the deep dark reason why
I am accounted frivolous.

I came back from the dead when I was four
with a brand-new voice to mark my resurrection.
It had a mocking sound to it, my mother said,
when it wasn't being miserable.
I was a funny little so-and-so, in her opinion.

I've never lost that sound, though often I have wanted to.
It was extinction's gift to me.
It camouflages every sorrow I've survived.

The Prelude

Poets were sissies when I was a kid.
They had nancy-boy feelings. They weren't like men.
It stood to reason.

Poets were scroungers when I was a kid.
They were poor as church mice. They lived off others.
You couldn't trust them.

Poets were layabouts when I was a kid.
They were born bone idle. They were less than useless.
Just heed the warning.

Poets were this and poets were that when I was a kid.
They weren't good people. They were not like us.
That was for certain.

Poets were worse than tarts when I was a kid.
They didn't have morals. They knew no shame.
They spread diseases.

The things I was told about poets when I was a kid
made them sound heavenly. I craved their strangeness,
their wilful disorder. I wanted to be like them
if it were possible.

I think I was told these things about poets when I was a kid
because the tellers loved me and cared for me
after their fashion.

Soap and Water

Imagine a shrimp of a boy encased in a skinny frame.
'His head's seldom out of a book,' he hears people say of him.
'He won't grow up to be big and strong if he carries on like that.'

He has a granny who never looks really clean to him,
not in the really clean way his mother looks really clean
or scrubbed to a shine like all but one of the nurses
who helped him to fight for his life when he was four years old.

It's a sunshiny day in the summer of 1944
and his dirty granny is telling him to put his skates on
and get out of bed, for there is serious work to be done.
She has a gentleman's body to wash.

Imagine a boy of seven puzzling over these words.
He washes himself, after all, as he's been taught to, over and over,
by his really clean mother, so why can't a gentleman do the same?
He asks his granny that question and she mumbles back
that curiosity killed the cat and beggars can't be choosers.

He's in the dark now with her talk of cats and beggars.
He'll ask the gentleman himself,
who'll tell him.

Or so he hopes as his granny takes him by the hand
to the very grand house at the top of the hilly street
which belongs, she says, to a family called Southampton.

'We're expecting you, Emily,' says the man who opens the door.
He's wearing a black suit and a black tie
which strikes the boy as a little bit funny
considering how hot it is already.
'Mr George is as ready, Emily, as he'll ever be
and waiting for your kind attention on the table.'

The boy is flustered. Why is this gentleman,
this Mr George, waiting on a table for a dirty old woman
to wash him? His granny smells of the snuff
she sniffs up her nose. It's given her a yellow moustache
that scrubbing can't get rid of.

'We've put him in the dining room, his favourite in the house.'
The man in black is smiling as he speaks.
'He loved his food and drink, did Mr George,'
says Emily. 'I waited on him many times.'

Imagine what the skinny shrimp sees next.
The dining room's enormous. So's the table, too,
that seems to stretch for miles. In its centre,
under a clean white sheet or tablecloth,
lies something bulky.

The man in black whisks off the sheet or cloth,
saying 'Hey presto, Emily!'

Imagine, if you can, the boy's surprise
the moment the gentleman's revealed. He wonders why
this Mr George forgot to dress that morning,
what made him settle for his birthday suit.

A maid brings in a bowl of water.
She puts it on the endless table.
Another carries towels, a flannel, and a slab of reddish soap
that's known as Lifebuoy.

The gentleman who liked his food and drink
does not even move when the dirty granny
starts washing his very fat and purply body.
'There's a lot of him to clean,' she says.
'God rest his soul.'

She cleans and wipes his chest and tummy,
his arms and legs and feet. It's time to turn him over,
she tells the man in black. A second man appears,
out of the shadows, to offer his assistance.
They have a struggle. 'Heave ho!' they say,
and Mr George is lying upside down
while dirty granny squeezes out the flannel
she's just used on his thingummy and balls.

The shrimp who's seven and six months
looks on as his dirty old granny –
who reeks of snuff and sweat and the stout
she's fond of drinking –
gives the gentleman a 'thorough scour'.
'He's made a motion,' she informs the man in black.
'They all do at the end. It's only natural.'

Imagine the little boy's state of mind
when he hears his dirty granny declare
'He's sweet and lovely for his Maker now'
as she sprays the body with lavender cologne.

He has witnessed something strange and thinks he knows
it has to be doing with death and not feeling free
to play in the sunshine.

That night, in his bed in dirty granny's cottage,
he hears himself crying softly for his very clean mother
who's in London hiding from the doodlebugs.

He wakes in the faintness before dawn. He's feeling happy
    and warm
before he becomes aware of his thingummy trickling.
He's done it again. The sheet is wet and so are his pyjamas.
He's a bad boy who has to be punished.
It's what he deserves, his granny will tell him
as she plunges his head into the wetness he's made
that she's sprinkled with pepper.

Imagine.

Passion

My father's rolling a cigarette. My mother's knitting.
There's silence between them, except for the clickety-clack
of her needles.

He pours himself another beer. She wonders why
without ever asking the question. He hears it even so
since he's alert to all the things she doesn't say.

It's now he calls her Woman. She loathes the word.
Woman, he snarls again. Be quiet, Woman.
She goes on knitting.

I'm in the corner, reading. Although I'm only ten
they've named me the Professor. Neither of them knows
how much I see of their unhappiness

as I look up from my book. I try to picture them
as they must have been once, desperate to clutch each other
like Romeo and Juliet in a place called Verona.

Love

I guessed my mother had mixed feelings about love.
She didn't really approve of it.

Love was something only fools had time for.
They had the money for it, she reminded me.

Whenever she mentioned love, it came with a question mark.
It was a word, I gathered, that needed consideration.

She was a widow when the subject of love first came up
between us. I ventured that she must have loved my dad.

'That's best not spoken of' was all she answered.

Ducklings

Whenever I felt the need to boast
about my achievements in school,
like being top of the class at French
or winning an essay prize,
my newly-widowed mum didn't mutter
'Pride comes before a fall',
as other, proverbially-minded, parents did
to their clever sons and daughters
who were blowing their own trumpets
to fill, as I was doing, an indifferent silence.

No, my mother preferred to inform me
that she'd heard little ducks fart before.
'I've heard little ducks fart before'
she repeated on cue even when I was praising
the brilliance of somebody else.

I've spent almost seventy Aprils
looking at ducklings on ponds and lakes
as they follow their mothers in neat procession.
I've strained to hear what my mother says she heard
but the sound of ducklings gently breaking wind
continues to elude me.

Essential Stationery

Arthur Rimbaud, scorning a pen or pencil,
dipped a finger in his sticky arsehole
and wrote a poem on a bistro's menu
in his own fresh shit.

Essential turd. Essential stationery.

My mother spent most of her life in service,
earning her crust from titled gentry
and strapped-for-cash old aristocrats.
They spoke a different language.
They seldom called a spade a spade.

There was a high-born lady, she remembered,
for whom she used to shop on Fridays.
The lady made a list of her requirements:
her special Floris soap, some talcum powder,
all manner of things for scullery and larder
and eggs, of course, and Normandy butter.
And always, scribbled as an afterthought –
And not forgetting the ESSENTIAL STATIONERY.

My mother never forgot to buy
the toilet paper of the softest kind
with which the lady wiped her precious bottom.

History does not reveal
if Rimbaud cleaned his finger with a napkin.

Betrayal

I didn't want to hear my mother say she loved me.
Her words were heartfelt, as were the tears she shed.
They made me disconcerted.

I didn't tell her that I didn't want the ordinary love
she was offering up at long, long last. How could I admit
to feeling disappointed and forsaken?

She'd put me in my place for all my life
and suddenly I knew that I'd been happy there –
as happy as Larry, whoever Larry was.

I didn't need the loving mother of convention.
It was her dark, tormented soul I cherished most.
She'd seen the worst in people and the worst in me,
and I was desolate.

Guests

They came to us in droves, our family's missing persons,
whenever we had cause to celebrate.
There seemed no end to them.

Late on Christ's birthday was their favoured time
to put in an appearance. The mention of one name
soon conjured up a multitude.

My father's deaf-mute father, dead at twenty-seven,
always beguiled me most, but once my dad had gone
his silent presence vanished.

Others remained and reappeared, like clockwork,
as soon as drink had resurrected them.
The room was crowded, suddenly,

with tiresome aunts and raffish uncles,
a saintly child God wanted for His own,
a skinflint cousin who amassed a fortune,

and many more besides. They only went away
when there was no one left to comment on
their failings and their secrets.

They're nowhere now, the lot of them. The one guest I retain
from all those ghostly visitations is my father's dad,
the tongue-tied carpenter who died too young.

Elegy

My sister said there should have been four of us,
but one was missing.

Was it a boy or a girl? Mum never said.
But then Mum never said anything, my sister said,
when it really mattered.

The one who should have made four of us
along with my brother, my sister and me
never came home when he or she, or she or he,
should have come home.

Whoever he was, or she was, he or she vanished
before I came into being late in my mum and dad's lives.

My sister said our mother never said
what really happened between her birth and mine.
But what she did say, in a sudden burst,
one night in a pub, after our dad was gone, was
that there should have been, God help her, four of us.

Ambrosia

My mother had no taste for fancy words,
yet here she was calling me a gallivanter.

What horrors was she thinking of when she remarked
'I don't know why you feel the need to gallivant'?

She knew the gerund, too. 'That smell behind your ears
tells me that you'll be gallivanting if I'm not mistaken.'

She often was. I led an innocent glowing life most evenings
listening to Beethoven, marvelling at Shakespeare,
hoping their world elsewhere was in my reach

But there were nights her gallivanter had more urgent needs,
as she suspected. Oh, she'd have been so surprised
when I gave up my cherry in a room in Vauxhall
to a Jamaican dancer. My memory is still composed
of spit and blood and Vaseline
and an indelible rapture.

And there it always was, in its chipped enamel dish,
the cold rice pudding she had lovingly prepared
to welcome my return from gallivanting.
'It says Ambrosia on the packet. God alone knows why.'

Summer of Love

Jimmy Buffett was singing about a drunk
who was wasting away again in Margaritaville
on every car radio that summer.
I heard it first in Bill's mom's Chevy convertible
and took to it at once. The song conveyed to me
a glorious, rhythmic desolation, a drowning-of-sorrows
set to a steady beat. It linked me to a boy
with whom, I imagined, I was fatally in love.

Bill offered to show me the real America.
He asked if I'd ever gone to a drive-in cinema
to catch a movie. That's how I got to see
Star Wars, which everybody was talking about
that summer. We sat in the Chevy, I remember,
drinking from cans of Michelob I'd bought
at the Knickerbocker Liquor Locker
in nearby Moorhead.

The little I saw of the inter-galactic fantasy
held no appeal for me. The boy in the driver's seat
was all I cared for. Oh, and the characters
had such ridiculous names, none sillier than
Obi-wan Kenobi, an owlish sage in a hooded robe
who spoke sepulchrally. But I warmed to the Princess Leia.
She seemed to be taking the piss out of the inexplicable
starry goings-on – I remember I thought that summer.

Bill's Mom took a shine to me, though she wondered why
I found her son, who'd never impressed her with his brains,
so interesting. 'I love him to bits,' she said. Me, too, Mrs S,
I didn't respond, before we set off in her Chevy, Bill and I, to
spend a weekend in Minneapolis – eating my first wild rice at
Charlie's and watching *She Stoops to Conquer* at the
Guthrie and snapping Scott Fitzgerald's birthplace in St Paul
that bygone summer.

The real America, Bill said, was something else. He grinned
as he invited me to join him for a drink at the raunchy
Pink Pussycat saloon in downtown Fargo. He parked the
Chevy outside the bar, placing a card in the rear window
his buddy Greg had bought by mail from the Church of Gospel
     Ministry
in faraway Chula Vista. It bore the message CLERGYMAN
     VISITING
in classy Gothic script. I seemed to be living a life I had never lived
before that summer.

There were cowboys in Stetsons lolling in the Pink Pussycat
that August evening. They were getting steadily schnockered
(the Norse, I learned, for 'drunk'), but none was drunker than
the purple-faced man who lurched towards our table.
Staring glassily at Bill, bourbon in hand, he tried and failed
to speak because his mouth was opening and closing
on unformed words. We waited. Then Bill told me that this goddam
     jerk,
this heap of shit, was his dad, would I believe it.

A doomed romance has its attractions – brevity being
one of them. Bill met an older woman with two small
kids who needed a father and he quietly ditched me.
He wrote much later to say that this was the last
I would hear from him. He was wiping his slate clean.
He had made a solemn promise to Laurette that he would
never – and he did mean never – go with another guy again.

I turned forty that year and hosted a belated birthday party
that summer. Bill helped me with the dishes when the guests
were gone and then, to my joyous surprise,
seduced me. Now I sometimes hear Jimmy Buffett's drunk
vainly searching for his lost shaker of salt, and I know for sure
that the radiant Leia is still taking the piss and that pompous
old sod Obi-wan Kenobi is still intoning. I remain in the dark
about Bill and Laurette and the nature of their lives
together, but I've often wondered if he was ever tempted
to smudge his pristine slate.

Three Scenes from the Midwest

Fargo, North Dakota, 1978

1

Mona Sullivan warned her children that she didn't want their sympathy. 'Pity,' she said firmly, 'I can do without. Tears won't keep anyone alive.' She made the sign of the cross, and urged each one of her 'problems' – Boyd, Jo Ann, and Franklin – to do likewise. 'The Heavenly Father will look after me. God and my bridge game will pull me through. He'll see to it that I get to play in the state tournament next month.' She caught her breath. Then, in a commanding whisper, she addressed her youngest son: 'Franklin, those roses you bought – take them away. Cut flowers are already half-dead. I hate the sight of falling petals.'

Franklin protested, gently: roses were her favourites – red, white, pink, whatever; in summer there was a bowl of them in every room in the house; he had chosen not just any roses but special ones, from the best florist in town; he had told Mr Holverson they were for a very important lady; he had meant well, she must know that. 'To hear you,' his mother interrupted, 'you'd think Franklin Sullivan had just fought his way through a long operation, instead of the person who has. Stop whining. A whine's not a fit tone of voice for a man in his twenties.'

'You have great courage, Mother.'

'If you must say such things, say them brightly. You make courage sound as if it didn't stand a chance.'

Boyd, Jo Ann, and Franklin were allowed to kiss their

mother goodbye. 'Call before you come again. I like to be prepared.'

They took the elevator down to the hospital lobby. 'It's her baby she loves the most,' said Jo Ann. She ruffled Franklin's hair. 'It was always that way and it always will be. She bothers with you, Frankie. She wants you to be someone. She leaves us to ourselves.' Boyd, who rarely spoke, said that this was one point on which he had to agree with his sister. 'I have to agree, Jo Ann,' he added, for emphasis.

Franklin listened. The conversation upstairs had unnerved him. He smiled back at his brother and sister.

'She thinks you're privileged, Frankie, because of your arm –'

'When was a withered arm, a godammed withered arm, a privilege?'

'It's a gift from her God. It's there to inspire you. She's told you often enough.'

Franklin nodded. He would return to St Luke's tomorrow, or very soon after, with a bunch of fresh roses.

2

'My kids,' I call them. There's something so cold, so icy frozen, about the word 'students'. To me they're just kids, with all the worries and cares and problems that kids have. I have kids myself – three of them, and I don't have to say it, but they are lovely, really lovely – and I know, being a mother, what boys and girls go through. I'm kind of an expert where kids are concerned.

I'm essentially, deep down, a very happy, contented person. I remember my Gram and what she used to say to me whenever I was in the dumps. 'Now then, Grumblegrumpkin,' she used to say, 'you just put a smile on that dear little face, or I'll sit right down and blub along with you.' Then I'd light up straight, I really would. No one can call me Grumblegrumpkin at this point in my life – I've made sure of that.

I care about my kids, I really do, I really do care. I'm more than a teacher to them. I'm a sort of counsellor too. I've never flunked a kid, you know. If I was – were, *were*, were, of course . . . If I were the mom of some kid who'd failed a course, I know I'd feel bad, I'd hurt, I'd be really hurting, to see my kid in such a failure situation.

I'm an identifier. I identify with those kids; I truly deep down identify. Teaching English isn't enough for me – words, if they mean anything, are about communication. The kids here in the Northwest can wait for Shakespeare, but they can't wait to express their innermost feelings. That's why I get them to freewrite. They're so insightful. I mean, they have *feelings*. As a feeling person myself, I can feel what they feel.

Why don't you come to my class? The kids would appreciate you and your crazy – my joke! – English accent. I'm going to read them a poem of Emily Dickinson's. My theory about Emily is that she was too much a loner. She needed one caring person to be needed by, and he wasn't there. If she'd had that someone her life would have been so different – complete; fulfilled; meaningful. Look at the snow! I love nature. I'm really into nature. I'm a nature person. Summer, spring, winter, fall . . . Ah, I love the changes, I really do . . .

3

As the first snow fell, she realised that she had forgotten to board up the martin house for the winter. Now it would become the property of sparrows. When the martins returned at the end of April they would swoop away from their old home. They resented intruders.

Sparrows and grackles seemed to be the only birds who could endure the cold. The others flew south – to Florida, to California. They took their brightness to places where the sun would enhance it. The drab ones remained.

The temperature had dropped below zero; a blizzard was expected. She would look out at it, at the snow whirling. She had every comfort in the house, and a good supply of liquor. There was steak in the freezer. Let the storm come.

She heard a faint buzz. A fly – a blue-backed fly – landed on her wrist. A lone survivor, she thought. 'Like me,' she said aloud. Flies lived in muck, yet when you looked at them closely you could see their beauty. *Her* fly's wings had a reddish tinge – blue, red, black; a small miracle. The fly, like the snake, was not considered one of God's creatures. In the First Lutheran Church you were never called upon to praise the fly. The snake meant great evil, and the fly meant disease. It was at its happiest in the garbage. God so loved the world that He made the fly to live in muck.

It seemed to be content on her wrist – her fly. Her arm ached, but she wouldn't move it. Drab sparrows – in whose fall there was providence – were fighting to enter the martin house. The summer was a long way off: sometime in the spring she would wash the martins' property free of the sparrows' common smell. A summer creature – a bright summer creature – was on her flesh.

It buzzed once more. It left her and ascended. Then it plummeted, as gracefully as any martin. She knew that its descent was its last act on God's earth: a final, graceful act.

She took the dead insect into the yard. She laid it carefully at the foot of the martin house. She removed her winter clothing and lay down beside it. There was a trace of red in the grey sky.

She shivered at first, but soon she was warm.

She did not feel the cold when it came again.

Snow fell throughout the night.

Ancestral Voices

There were the ones who said
'I shouldn't be doing this. It's against
my religion. I ought to stop right now.'

And there were those who said
'If my wife found out, she'd murder me.
She'd have me hung, drawn and quartered
and that's the truth.'

There were those who said, with a hint of menace,
'I never kiss. I draw the line at kissing.
Kissing is something you only do to girls, I reckon.'

And there were others who said
they'd regret what they were doing in the morning
while they were doing it. Yet they persevered,
bless them. They carried on – as if,
they sometimes said, there was to be
no tomorrow.

There were the ones who said they were
drunk as skunks, pissed as newts, totally
rat-arsed. It was funny, they said, the
things you did when the drink got the better
of you. It was if, I remember they said,
you'd forgotten to be the man
you thought you were. They were
that confused, they said. They blamed it
on the lager.

There were the ones who'd have you believe them
when they said, in the softest tones,
as if they were in the confessional,
that this was their very first time, honestly.
Then they proved, as the night progressed
in the deep, preferred, shameful darkness,
that they were lying.

Those dear, desperate, departed voices
still echo for me. Who hears them now?

Somebody must do. Somewhere.

French Letters

We lingered on Westminster Bridge that evening
to marvel at the filthy Thames below.
'I must be dull of soul,' said Dostoevsky David,
'because if that's a "sight so touching in its majesty",
I'm passing by.' We stayed on, even so,
to laugh at the majestic spectacle
of condoms floating on the river's surface.

'The French are famous for their correspondence,'
Michael observed. 'They must have lots of happy pen pals here.'
We went on laughing till the light grew dim.

'Why are they called French letters?' I remember asking.
David, who'd read The Brothers Karamazov at the age of twelve
and was now immersed in Goethe, was the one who answered.
'The French just aren't ashamed of sex the way we are.
They make love with the lights on and they're not repressed.'
We urged him to continue. 'How many brothels can you find
In Dickens, Austen and George Eliot?' The question stumped
    us.
The subject was beyond our comprehension.
'None, I should say. Balzac's got plenty of them. Zola, too.
And Guy de Maupassant writes of little else.
And then, of course, there's Proust.'

Of course there was. We nodded. David smiled,
acknowledging our ignorance.

We took ourselves in hand in 1952.
We three, we wicked three.

Michael went into business and I became an actor
for eight ramshackle years, while Dostoevsky David
went out suddenly
in one of those countries where he spoke the language.

Venetian

Paolo and I invented Italian words together. In Venice once,
at the end of a night of feasting, we heard ourselves
coining *goblondola*, after encountering
a gondolier who begged us to give him a blow-job.
We didn't oblige him, but we renamed his boat
as we tottered hysterically into Piazza San Marco:
E una goblondola, questa barca. We had to tell everyone
that Giuseppe didn't require *lire*, nothing so venal.
He wanted somebody's tongue, somebody's willing mouth
to take him briefly into paradise.

Golden

My bedside clock said it was five a.m.
and although it was dark outside
you, Freddy, were a luminous presence.

Why were you so suddenly golden?
I couldn't make sense of it, and that's why I laughed
at the beautiful, muscular, god-like sight of you.

Freddy, you never looked like this in life.
You always looked like death. You made an art of it,
exulting in your paleness.

Freddy, my skeletal friend, my daily reminder
of human destiny, what were you up to just now
making yourself desirable?

Dear long-dead Freddy, I heard myself beg of him,
please stop tormenting me, please be
half-bald again instead of flaxen-haired.

Then it was seven twenty-five and a faint winter light
told me you'd gone. Oh Freddy, don't come back.
Stay with my other cherished absentees.

In Memory

after Ungaretti

He was called Mohammed Ashrif
but I only discovered his name
after we were lovers

He had a Pakistani father
and a Glaswegian mother
whose accent he'd inherited

He revealed to me once
that he had no country.
He considered London his proper home
because nobody really noticed him there
and no one said he looked different

He was Peter when I met him,
the two of us pretending to admire
a window display in a shop
near Piccadilly Circus
where Peter was touting for trade

I was his client before I became his friend.
That's how it started between us

He'd had the Koran pumped into him
but his mum read only soppy love stories
about doctors and nurses doing daft things to each other
when she was left to herself
which wasn't often

And then one day he announced –
and it *was* an announcement –
that he had to be a natural man because
that's what Allah wanted

It was *decreed.*
He repeated the word.
It was *decreed.*

He vanished – for ever, I thought or imagined.
I would see no more
of the Peter who was Mohammed
with his beguiling –
to me, beguiling –
guttural-sounding voice

But there he was, eleven years later,
forlorn on the doorstep,
smoking a rolled cigarette and asking
if I felt in the mood for a bit of the old fun

It was as bad as being dead
was how he described the marriage
he was running away from.
There weren't enough miles in the world
to put between him and her, whose name
he wouldn't waste his breath on telling me –
no, not nearly enough,
not millions of miles enough

He showed me photos of his three wee kiddies –
twin daughters and a son with a walleye –

and said he'd miss them in wherever it was
he was heading for

Our afternoon's old fun
was shaded with the knowledge
of his lasting disappearance

And now
I sometimes think of his nameless wife
and the kiddies he abandoned
eighteen years ago

and wonder if Mohammed returned to them
or if he travelled instead to a place
where he could be Peter again
if he wanted to

Perhaps he's dead.
Perhaps he was travelling towards his death
when he stopped by that day
for a bit of the old fun

He continues to tell me
in dream after dream
that I was the only person

who ever really knew him

Lux aeterna

His name translates as Victor Light,
the man who came to comfort me
when there was only darkness in my days

Morning Departure

You were so neatly dressed that dull March morning
you might have been going to a feast.
Except you weren't. We knew too well you weren't.

You had a single destination. Nowhere else
was in your desolate diary. The cab was waiting
to take you from me, you inferred, for ever.

'I'm going out with style, I hope,' you said, as you bent down
to kiss me. 'I'm putting on a show. I'm even wearing
my two removable front teeth.'

And so you were, and so it was that day, when pain was
    telling you
it had more horrible surprises up its sleeve.
You'd had enough. Now was the time for brightness.

Brightness was what you conjured up that grim March
    morning.

Consequence

Your mother got the shakes and so did you.
Hers were the cause of yours. 'Only death
can still them now,' she whispered. 'And
I wish it would.'

After her funeral, you made new friends:
halves, quarters, miniatures
of gin. You had to buy them small
to hide them well.

She was choreic, you cirrhotic. There's
the blunt truth. She never touched a drop,
she boasted. So you became a shade
drowning her sorrows for her.

Design

after Bacovia

The morning after your death
I took the dog to the park.

It was late March.
If there were green shoots on the trees
I didn't see them.

Grief has a way of bleaching things
and shadowing them too.
The whiteness and blackness around me
had been patterned by loss.

Then, in the park, the ghosts appeared:
your fidgety mother with her useless hands
perpetually shaking;
my father, drained of colour,
chatting away to the voiceless.

The birds in the park were cackling crows
and squabbling magpies.
They formed a dissonant chorus.

Circe – our not-quite-collie,
not-quite-sheltie,
not-quite-greyhound –
ran for the ball I threw and threw
and threw for her,
her darting goldenness my one distraction.

Urban

The man in the next bed was screaming *oraş, oraş* –
the Romanian word for 'town'.

I had to wonder why a town was frightening him,
what terrors it contained.

From bald head to toes he resembled alabaster,
like a statue brought to life to die.

His screams became a whimper.
Then a nurse sedated me.

Waking, I saw three women holding candles,
lighting his path to a brighter, townless world.

Beauty

Surrogate son is tending surrogate father
in the infirmary of a London prison.
The year is 18-something. It's a squally April.
I'm at the bedside, too; paying my annual visit
to the most piteous of my surrogate friends.

The train is juddering into Marble Arch
when a woman's voice tells me I'm beautiful.
I look at her. She's black. She's vast.
Her eyes have so much light in them
I can't make out their colour.

I was rapt while I read; I was lost to the world;
I was how God would have me – beautiful, I hear.
Suddenly I know she thinks my book's the Bible.
I try to shake my head, but fail. Instead
I cover up the title with a hand, and grin.

Blank Page

I have gone to buy a new address book.

It will be a very slim volume.

I can't bear any longer to look at the crossings-out –
the last only two weeks ago.

I don't need to set down where you are and how
    I can reach you.

That in itself's a blessing.

Lyrical

Nadia, the nurse from Braşov, is cleaning my arse
with hygienic wipes.
We're in Ward 7 West of a London hospital
on an overcast summer afternoon
and I'm delighting in her company.
We're both in love with the melancholy poetry
of George Bacovia, which we're reciting to each other
as she dabs away down there.

We have a single poem in mind. It's called 'With You . . .'
and the 'you' is probably the beset Romanian people
he is addressing with such beauty.
He tells them it is good to be lonely and forgotten
and lost in this unfeeling place –
'this country, full of humour.'

It's in the last of his eight undying lines
that he adds the adjective 'sad'.
O sad country, full of humour, he found himself writing
at the dawn of a decade that held few promises of hope.
There would be terror to come.

Nadia puts on a new pair of rubber gloves
now that her task's completed.
She eases me into the protective underwear
I'll need in emergencies and then she shows me
some photos of her family back home.
Her mother has osteoporosis, she sighs.

She takes my hand and presses it. I offer her my thanks.
She has to go. Another patient's waiting.

Afterlife

Marjorie thinks I'm you, not me.
She calls me by your name. I've stopped
correcting her. Some might say
I've given up the ghost.

Marjorie knows that one of us is dead.
She asks how long it is since I passed on.
'Five years,' I answer. She tells me I'm
at rest now, with the saints and angels.

Marjorie dotes on animals. She believes
they're silent witnesses for God, spying
on our behaviour. Their once-dumb tongues
speak in that heaven I've gone to.

Marjorie's mad. Marjorie smells. Marjorie's
best avoided. I only meet her when
I'm turning corners. Then I hear
You're looking well, considering; and young.

Hamlet in Old Age

He wants to sleep. He wants to sleep and sleep –
and if, and when, he wakes, he wants to see
the world he knew before his need to sleep.

That's really all he wants – to sleep and sleep.
Nothing else matters. Nothing else will do
except the nothingness of dreamless sleep.

He wants his eyes to close and stay shut tight
until the world he knew before the need to sleep
beckons him back again.

The bed's prepared. The crisp white cotton sheets
are ready to contain him. It's late; it's dark.
It's time to sleep. It must be time to sleep.

Amazement

Our cats have finished playing for the day.
They've licked each other clean,
the jet-black Silvio and his marmalade brother Silas.
They're nestling snugly in a wooden basket,
stuffed with discarded vests and sweaters,
resting on top of an exquisite kilim,
a subtle design of green and pink and blue:
the one memento of an unhappy interlude
we laugh at now.

We're eating cheese and drinking wine
and watching an idiotic TV entertainment
of the kind we've been addicted to for most of thirty years.
The contestants have their own sweet lexicon.
Everything's 'amazing' to them. 'It's just *amazing*'
they reiterate. 'I'm living the dream!'
I only baulk, being a pedant of sorts,
when they substitute 'awesome' for 'amazing'.
Awesome, for me, means something wondrous,
like God to a believer.
Milton is awe-inspiring and so is Schubert,
or Billie Holiday or Ella,
but not the tin-eared warblers on display before us
on the unstoppable treadmill.

Why do we go on looking at this mind-chilling stuff?
It's our diversion. We're opera-goers, after all,
and see the best films and plays.

We're legal partners, which amazes us,
given the times we've lived through.
It's awesome, in its way, this act of eating cheese
and drinking wine, as the world keeps darkening.

ⒸB *editions*

Founded in 2007, CB editions publishes chiefly short
fiction and poetry. Writers published in translation
include Apollinaire, Andrzej Bursa, Joaquín Giannuzzi,
Gert Hofmann, Agota Kristof and Francis Ponge.

Books can be ordered from www.cbeditions.com.